The Boy Who Cried Wolf

with

The Donkey in the Lion's Skin

Illustrated by Val Biro

Award Publications Limited

There was once a boy who had a flock of sheep. All day long he watched over them, but nothing ever happened.

The villagers told
the boy to shout for help
if he saw a wolf. But he never
saw one. He was very bored.

One day the boy had an idea.

"Wolf! Wolf!"
he cried.
The men from the village ran up the hill to chase the wolf away.

But the men saw no wolf.
So they went back to the village.

"We must have scared it away," said one man. The boy laughed. He thought he was very clever to trick the men.

The next day the boy played the same trick. "Wolf! Wolf!" he shouted at the top of his voice.

Once again, the villagers ran to help. They yelled and waved sticks and swords.

Once again, the men did not see a wolf. But they did see the little boy laughing at them.

"You will cry wolf once too often," warned the eldest man. But the boy just laughed.

After a while the boy became tired of his trick. For a time things were quiet in the village.

Then one day a real wolf did appear. It was very hungry.
It snapped its teeth at the boy.

The boy ran to the village as fast as he could. "Wolf! Wolf!" he cried. "Wolf! Wolf!"

But the villagers ignored him. They thought he was playing a trick on them again.

The wolf ate up all the sheep. The boy learned a lesson that day. He never told a lie again.

The Donkey in the Lion's Skin

One day a donkey found a lion's skin lying on the ground. He sniffed it to make sure there was not a lion still inside it.
   Then he had an idea.

"I am not a brave donkey, but perhaps if people believe I am a lion they will think I am strong!" He put on the skin like a coat.

The donkey trotted down into the village square. The people could not believe their eyes. "Help! It is a lion!" they wailed.

The donkey thought what fun it was when everyone ran away in fright.

The donkey chased after them, but as he ran the lion's skin slipped off his back.

He tried to roar, but all that came out was: "HEE-HAW!"

The villagers saw he was not a lion after all. "We are not afraid of a donkey!" they cried.

They were angry that the donkey had tricked them.

Without the lion's skin, the donkey no longer felt brave. So he ran away as fast as his legs would carry him.